ATTENTION CURIOUS KIDS!

RANDOM AND INTERESTING FACTS

By
Jonny Katz

Table of Contents

Introduction

In this book you will find hundreds of facts, and answers to questions like:

What are "snoticles"?

What is the loudest land animal on earth?

Which snack food can be used to keep you warm?

Why should you never order popcorn in South Africa?

What was the first vegetable planted in space?

What is Fairy Floss?

What animal can run faster than a cheetah?

Which animal can testify in court?

Can a dog smell when you're afraid?

Who was Mayor Stubbs and why did he purr so much?

What are sprites, blue jets, and elves?

Astounding Animals

Sloths have a reputation for laziness - and they do get quite a bit of shut-eye. However, there are other animals who sleep even more than the sloth.

Koalas love to nap. In fact, the average koala sleeps about 22 hours per day - and if you wake one of these cute creatures from its rest, it can get quite angry.

Sloths come in second in the need-for-sleep category. Your typical sloth is so low on energy it sleeps 20 hours a day. A sloth has to rest up before it can do something active, like chewing or climbing down a tree.

Opossums like to rest up 18 or 19 hours before going out at night to search for food.
Other animals who sleep away most of the day (and night) are tigers, armadillos, little brown bats, and cats.

Your average house cat sleeps about 15 hours per day.

The goliath beetle found in African jungles can grow up to 6 inches (14 cm) long and when it flies, it sounds like a small aircraft.

Guinea pigs are active 20 hours a day.

A mouse can squeeze through a gap about the width of a pencil.

Surf's up! Did you know, Dogs, cats, pigs, goats, and even alpaca have learned how to surf.

Here's a funny one. If you see a swarm of bees, you can refer to them as a bike of bees. It's not because they ride bicycles. Bike is an old English word meaning colony or swarm.

Now for an interesting group name. A gathering of rattlesnakes is called a rhumba. (I wouldn't advise dancing with them.)

Polar bears are left-handed.

When you're out in the garden or at a park, keep your eyes open for an army of caterpillars or an army of ants. These tiny insects get their name from the fact that they're well-organized and work together as a group.

A group of ferrets is called a business.

Sheep have been known to grin. Smile at a sheep and it might smile back at you.

A group of geese is a gaggle. I'm sure this name came from the sound they make when gathered together. Interestingly, geese were considered sacred animals 4,000 years ago in ancient Egypt.

Flying squirrels don't fly, they glide - and they can glide over 150 feet. That's about the length of ten cars parked in a line.

At 189 years old, the oldest living animal on earth is a Seychelles giant tortoise named Jonathan.

Pandas have been known to fake pregnancy to get more food from zookeepers.

The only residents of Pig Beach in the Bahamas are swimming pigs.

When two wolfs mate, they stay together for the rest of their lives.

Playing with pets makes people happy and relaxed. (But you probably already knew this.)

When rabbits are happy, they jump, twist, and kick in the air. This is called binkying.

Rabbits are much happier when kept in pairs.

Catalina Island off the coast of California has a population of 150 buffalo. It all started with just a few brought to the island by Hollywood for a silent film.

Cows have best friends and like to hang out together.

An island off the coast of Japan is home to over a thousand wild rabbits that are so friendly, they'll eat right out of your hand. Some consider this place a "holiday resort for bunnies".

A group of giraffes is called a tower.

More people are killed by vending machines than sharks.

According to the World Health Organization, the deadliest animal in the world is not the shark, lion or deadly viper, but the tiny mosquito. Mosquitoes can be found in nearly every part of the world and outnumber all other animals, except ants and termites, and can carry deadly diseases.

The animal with the shortest lifespan is the mayfly, which lives just 24 hours.

A common garden snail has 14,000 teeth.

White-tailed jackrabbits can jump an astonishing 21 feet straight up in the air and can run up to 35 miles per hour.

Giraffes are the tallest land animal, reaching 19 feet high. (I guess this means a jackrabbit could jump over a giraffe.)

The smell of skunk spray is so powerful a human can smell it over 3 miles away.

A male ferret is called a hob, a female ferret is called a jill, and a baby is called a kit.
What is one obvious difference between a crocodile and an alligator? Alligators have a broad u-shaped snout while in crocodiles the snout is narrow and v-shaped.

The howler monkey is one of the loudest animals on land. Its calls can be heard from three miles away.

What's the difference between a camel and a dromedary? Camels include two species: the Bactrian camel and the dromedary. The major difference between the two is in the number of humps. A dromedary has one hump and a Bactrian camel (which we just call "a camel") has two.

When a domesticated ferret is extremely happy, it will make noises while leaping, running into things and generally acting wild. Some people call this the "Ferret War Dance".

Polar bears have jet black skin under their white fur coats.

The legs of an ostrich are so powerful, one mighty kick could kill a lion.

Koala fingerprints are almost identical to a human's.

When a ferret is angry or frightened, it hisses, making a sound much like a snake.

Grasshoppers hear with their stomachs.

A wild boar in Australia once stole 18 cans of beer from some campers, got drunk and picked a fight with a cow.

The national animal of Scotland is the unicorn.

Bite-Sized Facts About Food

People in the 1500s had some odd ideas about fun. The wealthy might surprise a guest by putting a live animal in their pie. I suppose this explains the Mother Goose poem, "Sing a Song of Sixpence" that includes:

"Four and twenty blackbirds baked in a pie.
When the pie was opened, the birds began to sing.
Wasn't that a dainty dish to set before the queen?"
(That must have been one huge pie. And one
hungry queen.)

Honey never has to be refrigerated and will never go bad.
Norwegians usually eat their hamburgers with a knife and fork.

Seaweed can have more protein than chicken.

The hottest chili in the world is the "Carolina Reaper".

Fruit gummies are coated with Carnuba wax, the same wax used on cars.

When cranberries are ripe, they bounce.

A watermelon is 92% water.

The sandwich was invented for John Montagu, the Earl of Sandwich (Sandwich is the name of an island owned by the British.). He loved playing cards so much he didn't want to leave the game to eat, so he ordered his servant to bring him food he could eat while playing. Either a servant or the cook came up with the brilliant idea of putting meat between two slices of bread. Ta-Daa! The sandwich was born.

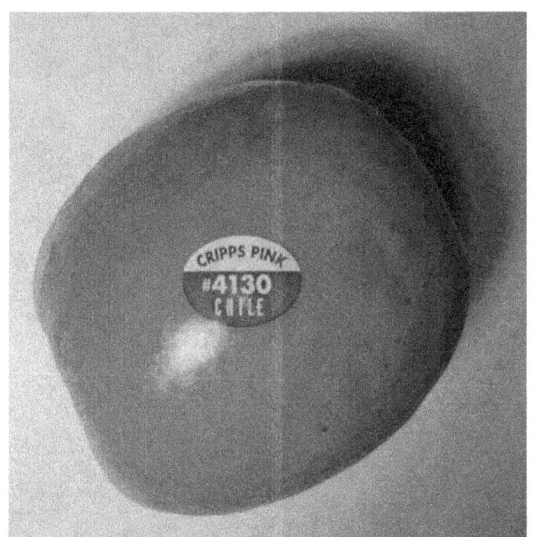

The stickers that you see on fruit and vegetables in the store are edible. They don't taste like anything, but they are safe to eat - although I wouldn't recommend it.

Ever thought about the difference between jelly and jam? Sure, you say, all the time. Well, here's the answer. Jam is made from fruit and jelly is made from fruit juice.

Salt, pepper, and chocolate were used at one time as money to pay for things, including salaries, rent, and taxes.

Gelatin is made from cow's and horse's hooves.

Cola drinks were also once sold as medicine.

The filling between the layers of a Kit Kat Bar is made up of … ground up Kit Kat Bars.

The most stolen food in the world is cheese.

Bananas, watermelons, kiwis, and cucumbers are classed as berries.

Ketchup used to be used as a medicine and was even sold as a pill.

White chocolate is not chocolate. It's just a sweet candy that is made with cocoa butter.

The red food dye coating red Skittles is made from crushed beetles. (Yum)

American cheese is not American. It was invented in Switzerland.

Doritos chips are flammable and can start a fire if you're in need of kindling. The oil and seasoning on the chips, especially the spicy varieties, can actually produce a reasonably long-lasting fire.

Fortune cookies were not originally made in China. They were invented in the early 1900s in San Francisco, California.

Most of us use refrigerators to keep our food cold, but Eskimos use theirs to keep their food from freezing.

MacDonald's once tried to sell kids on bubblegum-flavored broccoli. The kids they tested didn't fall for it.

Until Christopher Columbus began spreading plants and seeds around the world, there were no oranges in Florida, no bananas in Ecuador, no potatoes in Ireland, no coffee in Columbia and no pineapples in Hawaii.

Australians eat the most meat per person in the world. Americans come in second.

French fries were first made in Belgium.

German chocolate cake is not from Germany. It was created in Texas by an American baker named Samuel German.

The delicious dessert, pound cake, got its name from its original recipe: one pound of butter, one pound of eggs, and one pound of sugar. That must make a giant cake.

Peanuts have an oil that is used in making nitroglycerin, which is used in dynamite.

If you've ever tried eating Fruit Loops one by one, you probably noticed they are all the same flavor.

In ancient Egypt, workers were sometimes paid in radishes, onions, or garlic.

Next time you enjoy a plate of macaroni and cheese, give a quiet thanks to Thomas Jefferson. He brought the first macaroni and cheese over to the from France and also introduced the tasty dish to Americans.

Never order popcorn in South Africa. What they call popcorn is roasted termites and ants.

Want to test if an egg is fresh? Place it in a glass of cold water. A fresh egg will sink to the bottom - the fresher the egg, the quicker it sinks.

Popsicles were invented by accident. Story has it, an 11-year-old-boy named Frank Epperson left a cup of water mixed with soda outside on a cold night. By morning, it was frozen solid and tasted great. He named it an "Episicle". Later, when he became a dad, his kids called it the "popsicle" - and a summer favorite was born.

The lunch item, chimichanga, which you can find on most Mexican restaurant menus, does not come from Mexico. The dish was created in Tucson, Arizona. The name means "thingamajig" in English.

Apples are one-fourth air.

Cucumbers are 96% water.

Almonds are seeds, not nuts.

If you eat too many carrots, your skin can turn orange.

Carrots were originally purple - I guess if you ate too many of those, your skin would turn purple?

Popcorn was the first food to be microwaved.

Broccoli has more protein than steak.

Without plants, there would be no life on earth.

Potatoes were the first vegetables planted in space.

An ear of corn has an even number of rows - usually 16.

Grapes will explode in a microwave.

Candy Corn was originally called *Chicken Feed*.

The *Snickers* bar was named after a horse.

A dentist named William Morrison originally invented cotton candy. He called it *fairy floss*. (Not a great way to floss your teeth!)

M&Ms are named after Forrest Mars and Bruce Murrie, the two men who invented the candy. The *Mars Bar* was also invented by Forrest Mars.

The word candy comes from the ancient Indian word, khanda, and the Arabic word qandi, both of which mean "piece of sugar".

Tootsie Roll Industries

At one time, Tootsie Rolls were sold as a health food.

Curious About Canines

When exploring in the dark, a dog uses its whiskers to help perceive small changes in air currents. This gives them an additional way to know what's going on in their environment.

A dog's nose is always wet; this helps it absorb certain smells. Sometimes, the dog will lick its nose to taste what it had just smelled.

The nose print of a dog is so unique and detailed it can be used to identify a specific dog in the same way a human's fingerprints can identify a particular person.

Almost a quarter of all dogs snore in their sleep.

All dogs are descendants of wolves, which is probably where they got their great ability to howl.

Most dogs have paws that smell like corn chips. This phenomenon has been named "frito feet".

The United States is home to more dogs than any other country in the world. Second place in dog population is Brazil.

Dogs have keen senses which allow them to be aware of an approaching storm way before a human being can hear, see, or smell it.

Don't try to outrun a dog (or a cheetah). An average dog can run 19 miles per hour. An average human, 7.25 miles per hour. And your average cheetah? 74 miles per hour.

The most dogs ever owned by a single person was by Kublai Khan of the Mongol Empire. At one point, this dog lover had 5,000 mastiff dogs.

Dogs have a dominant paw, like humans have a dominant left or right hand.

An average dog can understand about 250 words or hand motions.

Not only do dogs pant to stay cool, they also sweat from the bottom of their paws.

A dog's sense of smell can be up to a million times better than a human's. The dog breeds with the best sense of smell are the bloodhound, the Basset hound, the Beagle and the German Shepherd.

Dogs have twice as many ear muscles as humans have and hear four times better.

Puppies learn from older dogs, so if you have a trained adult dog in your house, it becomes easier to train a new puppy.

Why do male dogs raise their leg when peeing? They want to make their mark as high as possible. This makes them appear larger to other dogs.

In the city of Paulding, Ohio, it's legal for a police officer to bite a barking dog. Yup. Weird, but true.

In Chicago, it's illegal to give whiskey to your dog. I guess beer and wine are okay?

It's against the law to make "ugly faces" at a dog in Oklahoma.

All breeds of dogs have pink tongues except for the Shar-Pei and the Chow Chow, which have black ones.

One of the dog breeds most related to the wolf is, believe it or not, the toy-sized Shih Tzu. The name Shih Tzu translates to "little lion".

Also in Oklahoma, dogs must have a permit signed by the mayor to gather in groups of three or more.

The Pekingese were so revered in ancient China that royal dogs of this breed had their own servants.

Some dogs are considered extremely valuable. In 2014, a Tibetan Mastiff sold for close to $2 million - the largest amount ever spent on the purchase of a dog.

The French Poodle originally comes from Germany.

The Australian Shepherd was first bred in America.

In 1941, a bomb was dropped through the roof of a house in England where a Great Dane named Juliana lived with her owner. Juliana peed on the bomb and put out the fire. For her heroism, she was awarded the Blue Cross medal.

The Hollywood movie star German Shepherd, Rin Tin Tin, signed contracts for 22 films with his paw prints. One of those films, won Rin Tin Tin an Academy Award nomination.

A group of dogs is usually called a kennel or a pack. However, because of the grunting and snorting sounds these dogs make, a group of pugs is called a grumble or grumbling.

At one time, people believed Great Danes could keep away evil spirits and ghosts.

The brilliant composer, Wolfgang Amadeus Mozart, once wrote a song dedicated to his pet dog, a Pomeranian named Pimperi.

Even though about 30% of Dalmatians are deaf in one ear; they can still hear better than humans.

Barry, the Saint Bernard, was the most successful search and rescue dog. He single-handedly (single-pawedly?) saved 40 people's lives.
The British Royal family have owned Pembroke Welsh Corgis for over 80 years.

When Dalmatians are born, they're pure white.

Seventy percent of people add their dog's 'signature' to greeting cards.

A dog's nose can sense heat and cold.

The Basenji breed of dog doesn't bark; it yodels.

If you yawn in front of your dog, it's likely to yawn too.

A person's blood pressure goes down when they're petting a dog - so does the dog's.

Dogs will act unselfishly and kindly without expecting a reward.

Although the cheetah is the fastest land animal, a greyhound can overtake a cheetah in a race that lasts over a minute. A cheetah can run twice as fast as a greyhound, but can keep that speed for only about 30 seconds.

The Bloodhound's sense of smell is so accurate that his findings can be used as evidence in a court of law.

The largest dog in the world was a mastiff named Zorba. Zorba was over 8 feet long from nose to tail and weighed 343 pounds.

U.S. President Lyndon Johnson had two Beagles, one named Him and one named Her.

France has one of the highest dog populations in the world.

Dogs can smell the faint odor of sweat when a person is afraid.

87% of dog owners watch TV with their canine friends.

One million dogs have inherited money from their owners.

Just like hair on people, the fur on older dogs can turn gray as they age.

Dogs have been used to help the police track down criminals and find evidence since the 1800s.

A third of all households in the world have at least one dog.

Over a third of Americans have talked to their dogs on the phone or left them voice messages.

Maximus Mighty-Dog Mueller II is the official mayor of the town of Idyllwild, California. He is the son of the first canine mayor of the town, Mayor Max.

U.S. President Teddy Roosevelt had a dog named Pete who ripped a French Ambassador's pants off at the White House.

In Russia, stray dogs have learned to use the subway system, getting off at the same stops each day. (I imagine they ride for free.)

An elderly woman in Korea went out one day with her dog Baekgu. The woman lost her way and collapsed in a field. Baekgu never left her side and lay on top of her to keep her warm when it rained. Rescuers sent out a drone which discovered their location. In celebration of finding the woman and of Baekgu's loyalty and bravery, a party was held and Baekgu was rewarded with cake, flowers, and a new home for him and his owner. Baekgu also became Korea's first honorary rescue dog.

The smallest dog was "Miracle Milly" who was 3.8 inches tall when she was born and weighed 1 pound.

The scientific name for a dog is "canis lupus familiaris". Canis is the Latin word for dog. Lupus in Latin is wolf. Familiaris means "a member of the family". But I think we might as well stick to calling these furry friends "dogs".

A German Shepherd named Gavel was trained from the time he was a pup to be a police dog. He was smart, a quick-learner, and good at all the details of his job as a police dog. However, there was one problem. Gavel loved people, all people, even criminals. And so, he was fired from his job as a police dog and given a new one as the Vice-Regal Dog for Queensland, Australia. He now lives at the governor's mansion and gives tours to visitors.

We know that dogs will obey orders like sit and stay. But did you know an average smart dog can learn around

165 words? Many dogs have also been taught to follow written commands, such as jump and speak. They learn to recognize the shapes of the words, which is a simple kind of reading.

Facts to Count on

There are 31,557,600 seconds in a year.

There are 42 Quintillion possible combinations on the Rubik's Cube - but only one is correct.

Arithmophobia means fear of numbers.

The opposite numbers on a die (one of a pair of dice) always add up to seven.

Four is the only number that has the same number of letters (in English) as its value.

Zero is the only number that can't be written in Roman Numerals.

Jeremy Harper of Alabama holds the Guinness World Record as the fastest person to count to a million. It took him 89 days. He recorded himself counting aloud 16 hours a day and sleeping and eating the other 8.

The word love in tennis means a score of zero.

By the time you finish all the verses, the total number of gifts given in the song "The Twelve Days of Christmas" is 364.

Zero is an even number.

The city of Denver, Colorado is called the "Mile High" city. And it is at precisely 5,280 feet elevation - that's exactly the length of a mile.

Most months of the year (7 out of 12) have 31 days.

If you put a single grain of rice on the first square of a chessboard and then two on the next, then four, and kept doubling the previous number of grains, by the time you got to the last square, you would have enough rice to cover an entire country. This is called "exponential growth".

A googol is one followed by 100 zeros.
There's a French riddle that has to do with this idea of exponential growth. A lily pond starts with one leaf. Each day, the number of leaves double - two on the second day, then four, then eight; and so on. If the pond is entirely full on the 30th day, on which day is the pond half full? (29th Day)

Our system of telling time with 60 seconds in a minute and 60 minutes in an hour comes from the Babylonian counting system used over 4,000 years ago.

Forty is the only number in the English language whose letters are in alphabetical order.

The famous mathematician Descartes invented the system we use for drawing graphs, using x and y axes after watching a fly crawl around the ceiling of his bedroom as he lay in bed.

A tribe in Brazil has only words for one, two, and many. So, members if the tribe can't count three or more objects.

A billion is a one followed by nine zeros. It's a thousand million.

The speed of a computer mouse is measured in Mickeys (named after you-know-who). A Mickey is 1/200th of an inch.

From Purrs to Roars–All About Cats

One of the names for a group of cats is a glaring.

The definition of glaring is "having a fixed look of anger, fierceness, or hostility". Anyone who has had a pet cat has seen that look in their eyes.

If you meet up with a group of wild cats, first, get the heck out of there, and then you can tell people you saw a "destruction" of cats.

A group of kittens is called a litter or an intrigue.

A cat can run at a top speed of 31 miles per hour (49 km) over a short distance.
A group of tigers is called a streak, an ambush, or a hide.

A cat's heart beats nearly twice as fast as a human heart.

A cat can jump up to five times its own height in a single bound.

You can refer to lions as a pride or a troop.

The name of a gathering of jaguars sounds like fun. A group of these members of the cat family is called a jamboree.

Leopards come in leaps and a group of cheetahs is a coalition.

A lion's roar can be heard 5 miles away.

Cats are the most popular pet in the United States.

More than 88 million cats are kept as pets in the U.S.

Cats have 30 muscles that control their ears; humans have only 6.

A cat can rotate its ears 180 degrees. (That's all the way from side to side.) They can also move their ears separately.

Cats are such sleepy heads, they spend 70% of their time sleeping.

Cat noses are as individual and unique as human fingerprints

A cat called Stubbs was mayor of Talkeetna, Alaska, for 15 years.

A cat ran for mayor in Mexico City in 2013, but lost to one of those pesky humans.

A cat's purr has healing powers. A domestic cat's purr has a sound frequency that can help muscles and bones grow and repair themselves.

Cats have unique meows, each cat developing its meow to best communicate with its owner and other humans. Listen to a few cats "talk" and you'll hear the many differences in their meows.

Adult cats only use their meows to "talk" to humans, not each other. The only time they mew to communicate with another cat is when they're kittens and are getting the attention of their mothers. Cats will make other sounds like trills, chittering, yowls, and growls to communicate to other cats. In fact, a cat can make around 100 distinct sounds; dogs make only about 10.

According to the Guinness Book of World Records, the longest living cat was Creme Puff of Austin, Texas, who lived to the age of 38 years and 3 days.

Polydactyl or "mitten-pawed" cats have one or two extra toes on each of their paws.

These cats are sometimes called "Hemingway Cats" because the famous writer Ernest Hemingway owned dozens of them at his home in Key West, Florida. Hemingway's first "mitten-pawed" friend was a completely white cat given to him by a ship's captain who believed, as many sailors do, that cats with extra toes brought good luck. Ernest Hemingway's son named the cat Snow White.

U.S. President Theodore Roosevelt kept a polydactyl "First Cat" named Slippers.

Scientists have done studies which show owning a cat is good for your health.

Sir Isaac Newton invented the first cat door or cat flap to keep his cat "Spithead" from opening or scratching at the door and ruining his experiments.

A cat's strongest sense is its sense of smell, which is 14 times better than a person's. The cat uses smell to identify people, other animals, plants and objects.

The Maine Coon breed of cat is often found with extra toes on its paws. They use their large paws and extra toes like snowshoes to help keep them from sinking into the snow.

The average cat can jump as much as 8 feet in a single bound.

A female cat is sometimes called a "molly" or a "queen".

A male cat is often referred to as a "tom" or "tomcat".

The ancient Egyptians were so attached to their cats that when one died, the owner would shave their eyebrows to show grief.

In Japan cats are thought to turn into super spirits when they die.

Most cats are left-pawed.

Cats don't like fighting and will go out of their way to avoid one another in order to prevent a disagreement.

Cats can detect earthquake tremors 10 or 15 minutes before humans can.

Cats have an amazing sense of balance.

Cats spend nearly 1/3 of their waking hours cleaning themselves.

A cat has more bones in its body (230) than a human does (206).

A cat named Towser has a tower in Scotland dedicated to her for having caught 30,000 mice.

When a cat leaves a dead animal in the house, she is fulfilling her role as a hunter and a friend.

The little tufts are fur inside a cat's ear are called "ear furnishings".

In the original Italian version of Cinderella, the fairy godmother was a cat.

The first cat in space was a French cat named Felicette (nicknamed Astrocat). The cat blasted off into space in October 1963. She returned home safely in her small rocket after a 15-minute orbit of earth. She was honored 54 years later with her own bronze statue at the International Space University in France.

According to an old legend, cats were created when a lion on Noah's ark sneezed and two kittens came out.

Cats use their whiskers to find out if they can fit through a space.

The wealthiest cat in the world is Blackie, who inherited $12.5 million from his millionaire owner, a man named Ben Rae. The rest of Mr. Rae's fortune went to cat charities. Interestingly, Ben's sister Dorothy must have liked cats, too. She left her $5 million to animal charities.

The fastest land animal is the Cheetah. This member of the cat family can get from zero to 40 miles an hour in just three strides. And it reaches a top speed of a little over 70 miles an hour—which would break the speed limit on most roads and many highways.

New Zealand has more cats per person than any other country in the world. Close to half of all households own at least one cat.

Quilty, a 6-year-old shelter cat learned how to get out of his cage and open cage doors to let out all his kitty pals during the night. The shelter posted a picture of Quilty on its Facebook page asking for someone to adopt this rascally feline. They received messages from dozens of cat-lovers and Quilty was adopted within hours of the posting.

Fun Facts About Toys

The word toy comes from an old English word meaning "tool".

The first doll house was made for the Duke of Bavaria in 1557 and was a copy of his own home.

Erno Rubik invented his cube by accident.

One of the first jigsaw puzzles was created in 1760 by a mapmaker. The puzzle was a wooden board with countries cut out and was made to teach children geography.

An America woman named Charlotte Lee has the largest collection of rubber ducks in the world - 5,631.

The game of marbles goes back over 5,000 years and was played by ancient Egyptians and Greeks.

Play-Doh was originally invented as wall paper cleaner.

One of the first toys invented was the spinning top.

The Yo-Yo is another ancient toy, played with by Greek children over 2500 years ago.

In the Philippines, during the 16th century, the Yo-Yo was used as a hunting weapon.

The current Frisbee sold in toy stores and tossed around in parks all over the world, had its beginnings as a pie tin used by the Frisbee Pie Company.

The Barbie doll was named after the daughter of Ruth Handler, the woman who invented the doll. Barbie's full name is Barbara Millicent Roberts. Ruth's husband,

Elliot Handler, invented the Ken doll two years later and named him after their son.

Since Barbie's boyfriend, Ken, was invented, he has held over 40 occupations. Barbie has had over 150 careers - from registered nurse to rock star, veterinarian to police officer.

Barbie has seven brothers and sisters: Skipper, Todd, Tutti, Stacey, Kelly, Chelsea, and Krissy.

Kites originated in China, but they were not toys. Around 1200 BC, the Chinese military used them as signaling devices. The color of the kite, its patterns and even the way it moved all communicated coded messages.

LEGO is the world's largest tire manufacturer. The company makes over 300 million tires a year - lots more than Goodyear!

Why do People Save Money in a Piggy Bank?

Pigs have never been known to store food for the winter or open a savings account, so why do we save change in a piggy bank?

During the Middle Ages, dishes and pots were made from a cheap clay called pygg. Whenever someone had an extra coin, they'd toss it into a clay jar they called their pygg or pyggy.

Hundreds of years later, this type of clay was no longer used. When a potter was asked to make a "pyggy bank" he thought the customer meant a "piggy bank" and created the little savings container we know now. And so, the tradition was born.

The word "Crayola" comes from two French words; one meaning chalk and the other meaning oily. So, really a crayon is a piece of oily chalk.

The toy "Furbies" was banned from the National Security Agency headquarters in Maryland because the agency thought they would "listen in" on top-secret conversations and repeat what they heard. "Furbies" could not record anything and were not secret agents from a foreign country.

The Little Tike's Cozy Coupe was the best-selling car in America in 1991; it even sold more than popular cars from Honda or Ford.

The modern Hula Hoop was originally inspired by a bamboo exercise ring used in Australia during gym classes.

The two people who did the cartoon voices for Mickey Mouse and Minnie Mouse fell in love and got married.

The patient's name in the board game "Operation" is Cavity Sam.

It takes 80 feet of wire to make one Slinky.

The very first Easy Bake Oven was turquoise.

The first popular video game was called Pong. It was based on the game of table tennis.

In 1943, a pigeon named G.I. Joe saved the lives of over 1,000 people in a small Italian village. When the company Hasbro was looking for a name for their military action figure toy, someone thought of naming it after that hero pigeon from World War II.

John Lloyd Wright, the son of the famous architect Frank Lloyd Wright, invented Lincoln Logs.

The Teddy Bear was named after U.S. president Theodore Roosevelt.

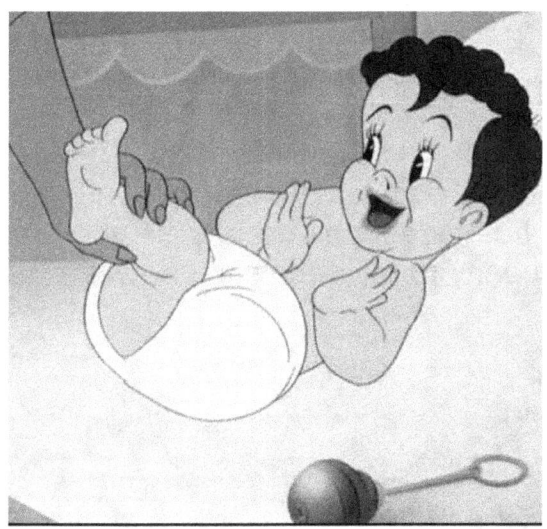

One of the oldest toys in the world is the baby rattle.

Candy Land was invented by a woman named Eleanor Abbot while she was recovering from polio in a San Diego, California hospital. She created the game to help entertain and distract the children who were with her in the ward.

The toy Stretch Armstrong gets his stretchiness from boiled down corn syrup.

When Mr. Potato Head first came out, he had no head. Kids were given a bag of plastic eyes, noses, and mouths. Parents supplied the head in the form of a real potato.

Mr. Potato Head has a family - Mrs. Potato Head, and two children, Brother Spud and Sister Yam. The original toy also had vegetable chums like Katie the Carrot, Pete the Pepper, and Cookie the Cucumber.

The Super Soaker was invented by a NASA engineer who also helped develop the stealth bomber. He used the money he made from selling the Super Soaker to open a company to research solar power.

It's tough to balance on an original pair of roller skates.

The first pair of roller skates were modeled after ice skates and had only two wheels in the center of the bottom of each skate. The inventor, a Belgian musical instrument maker, made them to wear at a costume party. Unfortunately, he never practiced how to stop and when he arrived, he rolled into lots of guests before crashing into a mirror and falling on his butt.

In 1950, the Gilbert Toy Company came out with a rather frightening science kit called the U-238 Atomic Energy lab. This toy contained real uranium and was radioactive. It's now thought of as the most dangerous toy ever made.

The most common plaything used by children around the world, since the earliest of times, is the simple stick. A baseball bat, hockey stick, pool cue, and even a bow and arrow started out as a piece of wood - or stick. This is why in 2008, the stick proudly joined Barbie, Slinky, the Yo-Yo, Mr. Potato Head and others in the Toy Hall of Fame in Rochester, New York.

The oldest known rocking horse was owned by King Charles I of England.

Giant Facts About Elephants

Elephants use their ears as fans, waving them back and forth to cool off in the African heat.

An elephant's ear can be six feet long and weigh a hundred pounds.

Elephants greet each other with their trunks - like they're shaking hands.

Even though elephants are the largest land animal in the world, they are afraid of ants.

Elephants can hold up to 4 gallons of water in their trunks at one time.
The trunk of an elephant is strong enough to be used to push down trees and also delicate enough to pick up a single piece of straw.

Like rabbits and cats, elephants are born blind.

A baby elephant often holds its mother's tail as it walks until it can see.

Elephants have great memories and can recognize each other, even they haven't seen each other in years.

Elephants spend about 15 hours per day eating and, in that time, they consume about 300 pounds of vegetation.

In the world of elephants, the oldest female leads the herd. All the elephants in a herd work together to raise the young and protect them from danger.

A group of elephants is called a parade.

Elephants cannot jump.

Baby elephants suck their trunks for security in the same way baby humans suck their thumbs.

An elephant's trunk is called a proboscis.

Elephants don't like peanuts.

African elephants can sense water sources from up to 12 miles away.

Elephants sleep about half the time on their feet and half on their sides.

A new born elephant can weight up to 260 pounds.

Interesting Science

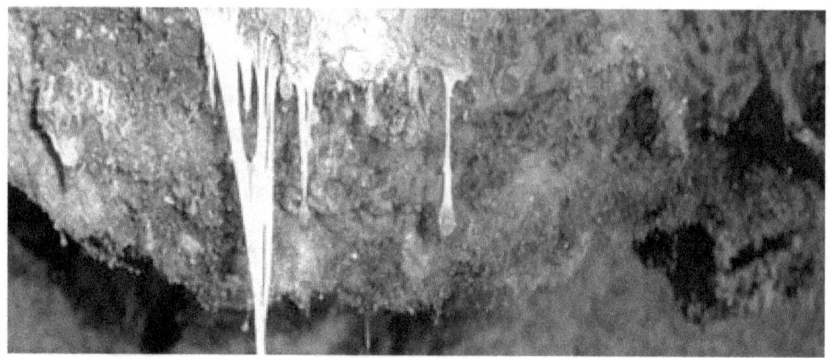
Snoticles

Deep inside some of the darkest caves, where almost nothing can survive, certain bacteria form a slimy film on the walls and ceilings. When the slime on the ceiling gets really thick, it drips. Scientists call these drips, snoticles or snottites. I bet you can guess why.

The Milky Way Galaxy is thought to be around 13.2 billion years old.

Nuclear power produces around 13% of the world's electricity.

Solar energy is made from sunlight.

Wind power has been used for thousands of years.

Around 100 countries use wind power to generate electricity.

Windmills are an example of using wind power.

The largest meteorite ever found weighed over 60 tons.

Stars appear to twinkle because of changes in the Earth's atmosphere.

Distances between stars are measured in *light years*.

The galaxy nearest our own Milky Way is the Andromeda galaxy.

The world's largest pearl, the Pearl of Lao Tzu, is about the size of a soccer ball.

All the gold mined in a year would fit inside an average living room.

Because high temperatures make iron expand, the Eiffel Tower can grow over six inches during the summer.

If you put a lime and a lemon in a bowl of water, the lime will sink and the lemon will float. Limes are denser than lemons, which makes them heavier.

A comet is a ball of ice and dust.

Tomatoes and avocados are fruit, not vegetables.

Earth is not a sphere; it bulges in the middle.

Once it's in space, a satellite uses very little energy—about as much as two ordinary light bulbs.

There is no sound on the moon because there is no air to carry sound.

Only 12 people have walked on the surface of the moon.

We only see one side of the moon from earth.

No new water is ever made in the atmosphere. The existing water recycles again and again. You could take your next a bath with water that once fell upon a dinosaur or was used to wash the hair of a princess.

Sprites, Blue Jets, and Elves are all types of lightning.

The hottest temperature ever recorded on earth was 134 degrees. This was measured in July, 1913 in the well-named town of Furnace Creek located in California's Death Valley.

The world's biggest snowflake was 15 inches wide and 8 inches thick.

A hailstone the size of a bowling ball fell in South Dakota in 2010.

Thunder is one of nature's loudest sounds.

A bolt of lightning is around 4 times hotter than the surface of the sun.

The United Kingdom has basic weather records dating back to 55 BC.

If you can hear thunder, you are within about 10 miles of a storm.

Bamboo can grow up to 3 feet (90 cm) a day.

Avalanches can reach speeds of 130 kilometers per hour. That's 80.77 mph.

Trees grow from the top–so, if you carve your name into the trunk of a tree, it will be there at the same height decades later.

The largest uncut diamond in the world is called the Cullinan. It was named after Cullinan, South Africa, the place where it was discovered in 1905. The stone is near colorless, 3,106.75 carats (1.37 pounds) and was sent as a gift to King Edward VII of England for his 66th birthday.

The biggest diamond cut from the Cullinan is known as the Star of Africa.

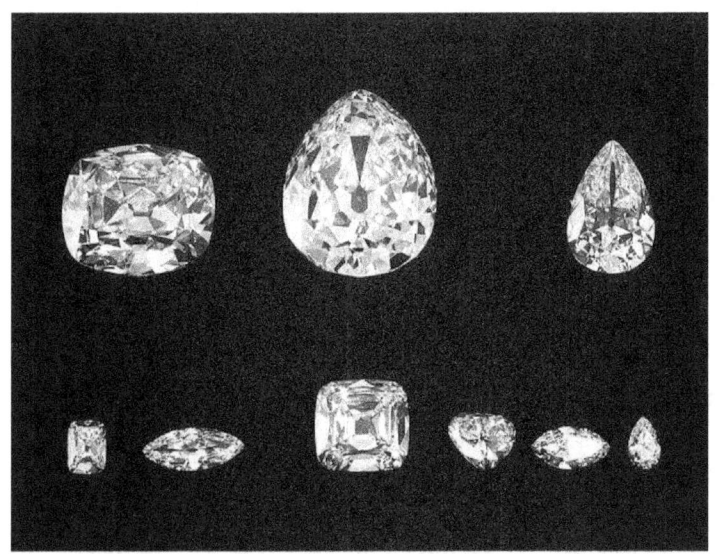

The Cullinan stone was polished and cut into two large diamonds and 96 smaller ones.

The tallest LEGO tower, built of 550,000 bricks was erected in Milan, Italy and completed in June 2015. It stands 35.05 meters (114 feet, 11 inches) - over 10 stories high.

Mosquitos are drawn to people who have recently eaten bananas.

When it comes to world records, South America can brag about quite a few:

The world's longest mountain range - The Andes, which reach from Venezuela to Chile.

The highest waterfall in the world- Angel Falls in Venezuela.

Largest tropical rain forest - The Amazon. It covers eight countries: Peru, Bolivia, Ecuador, Venezuela, Columbia, Suriname, Guyana, and over half of Brazil.

The driest hot desert is the Atacama in southern Peru and northern Chile.

The Atacama has mummies that are older than the Egyptian pyramids, snakes that grow up to 30 feet long, and spiders the size of dinner plates.

Living in the South American country of Columbia you will find The Poison Dart Frog, one of the tiniest (just 2 inches long) and deadliest frogs on earth. Even touching one of these frogs can cause death in less than ten minutes.

The Law Code of Hammurabi, King of Babylon, is nearly 4,000 years old, the oldest set of laws ever written.

Australia is home to the greatest number of species with the most lethal venom including: the box jellyfish, marbled cone snail, blue-ringed octopus, tunnel spider, and stonefish.

The world's most poisonous snake is the taipan. This reptile lives in the middle of Australia. Its venom is so powerful, one drop can kill 100 people.

The biggest rock in the world, Uluru, also known as Ayers Rock, is located in Australia. This landmark is more than 1,100 feet high and almost 6 miles around.

Australian Camel

The largest population of camels is not found in Arabia or Tasmania, the traditional homes of wild camels, but in Australia.

The only planet not named after a god is earth.

Hot and cold water sound different when poured. You can hear it if you listen carefully.

The hardest natural substance in the world is a diamond.

The purest air in the world can be found in Tasmania, an island south of Australia.

A single bolt of lightning contains enough energy to cook 100,000 pieces of toast.

The longest earthquake known lasted for 38 days.

The biggest cactus is the Saguaro, found in the Sonoran Desert in the southwest part of the United States. It can grow to be 50 ft. (15 meters) high.

Here's a strange fact... cold water heats faster than hot water. This is known as the Mpemba effect. Try it.

Raindrops fall at a speed of 11 kilometers (6.8 miles) per hour.

The rarest diamonds are blue or pink.

The smallest of the seven continents of earth is Australia (which is also the sixth largest country)

Rubies are the rarest gems in the world.

Bacteria are the oldest living things on earth.

Here's a trick question to ask a friend. What's the largest desert on earth? Most people would think of the Sahara, the Arabian Desert, or the Gobi. These three only rank 3,4, and 5 on the list. The two largest are the cold polar deserts. The Arctic and the Antarctic hold the number 1 and number 2 positions on the list. (A desert is a large area of land that gets little rain, making it difficult for plant and animal life to survive.)

Music and Art

Pablo Picasso could draw before he could walk.

The first pop music video was "Bohemian Rhapsody" by the group Queen in 1975.

Leonardo da Vinci's painting, of "The Mona Lisa" receives so many love letters it has its own mailbox in the Louvre.

Picasso's first word was lapiz, (pencil in Spanish).

Pablo Picasso loved animals and had lots of pets, including a monkey, a turtle, an owl, a goat, and many dogs and cats.

Beethoven wrote many of his most popular works after he was deaf.

The first animated feature film was not "Snow White and the Seven Dwarfs" or any other Disney movie. According to the Guinness Book of World Records, the first animated feature film was a full-length movie made in Argentina 20 years before Disney's first release. The film was called "El Apostol" and was made up of 58,000 drawings.

Elvis Presley failed one subject in high school - music.

Greece has the longest national anthem-58 verses.

Elvis Presley didn't write any of his own hits. He wrote very few songs at all.

Leonardo da Vinci loved animals and would even buy caged birds just to set them free.

Art used to be an Olympic event.

Famous street artist Banksy once hung his own work in London's Tate Museum.

Andy Warhol made 32 paintings of soup cans.

Music is played on all seven continents.

Ludwig Von Beethoven wrote a famous piece of music called "For Elise". No one has ever discovered who Elise was.

Michael Jackson was awarded 26 American Music Awards, 40 Billboard Awards, 13 Grammy Awards, and 23 Guinness World Records.

In 2016, classical composer Mozart sold more CDs than Beyonce - and that's a lot of CDs.

Plants grow faster and bigger when music is being played.

None of the Beatles could read or write music - I guess they still did okay.

A third of all country songs mention crying.

Michael Jackson was only 5 years old when he began performing with his brothers in the group called, "The Jackson 5".

Monaco has a military orchestra that is bigger than its army.

Cows relax and produce more milk when they listen to music.

Listening to music is good for your heart.

Happy Birthday to You is sung more often around the world than any other song.

The world's longest piece of music is still being performed live in Germany. It's called, "As Slow as Possible" and was written by composer John Cage. The performance of the piece began in 2001 and will continue until 2064.

In 1965, Jingle Bells became the first song to be performed in space.

The theremin is an electronic instrument that can be played without touching it.

Beethoven never learned how to multiply or divide. But he knew how to add and subtract. Once, when he needed to multiply 62 by 50, he wrote 62 down a line 50 times and added them all up.

There's a species of fly named after Beyonce'.

August 24th is International Strange Music Day.

In 2006, Sega Toys made the world's smallest playable piano. It is an exact copy of a normal piano, but only 25 centimeters (9.84 inches) wide, instead of the usual 5 feet.

Wolfgang Amadeus Mozart composed his first symphony at 8 years old and his first opera at the age of 11.

On and Under the Sea

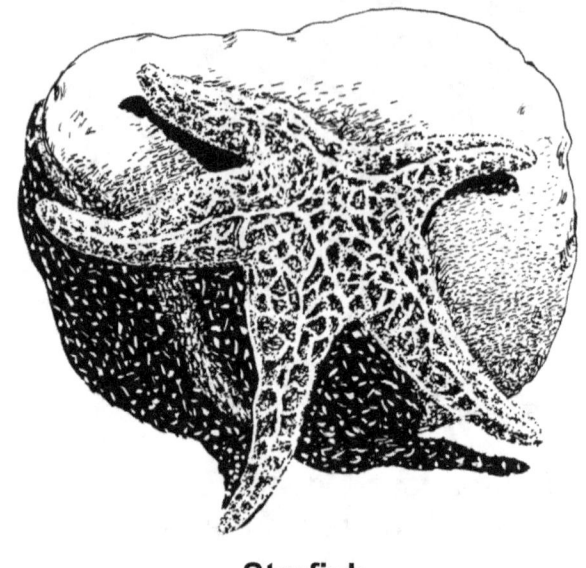

Starfish

Starfish and jellyfish are not really fish.

Goldfish can live up to 43 years.

A baby seahorse is called a fry.

The oldest known koi fish lived to be 226 years old.

Jellyfish don't have hearts, bones, or brains.

Most of us have heard of a "School of Fish". Here are some names for individual groups of sea animals:

A herd of seahorses
A company of angelfish
A family of sardines
A fleet of bass
A float of tuna
An army of herrings
A school of cod
A glide of flying fish
A squad of squid
A troop of dogfish
A troupe of shrimp
A swarm of eels

Lungfish can live out of water for several years. One of the oldest known fish is an Australian lungfish. It was still alive at 65 years old. (And may still be living today.)

Sharks are the only fish with eyelids.

Bluefin tuna can swim at 56 miles per hour.

The word "halibut" means "holy flatfish" because it was only eaten on Sundays.

Flying fish can launch themselves out of the water and glide in the air almost seven hundred feet - the length of about seven basketball courts.

Penguins can jump up to 10 feet straight out of the water and onto ice.

Just like dogs, penguins pant to stay cool.

This is weird. In ancient Greece, dentists used stingray venom to numb their patients.

A group of stingrays is called a fever.

Sea otters carry rocks in a pocket under their arms. They use the rocks to open clams.

Scientists have created a robot that looks like a jellyfish. Someday, they hope to send it out on underwater spy missions.

Seahorse couples dance together every morning, sometimes with their tails entwined so they won't lose each other.

Ocean plants produce more than half of the earth's oxygen.

Never whistle on a warship; according to old superstition, this can cause dangerous winds.

Ever wonder how the data you enter in your computer at home can reach someone thousands of miles away in a matter of minutes? One way it does this is through wires strung across the bottom of the ocean floor. There are over 750,000 miles of these wires, enough to circle the earth 30 times.

Next time you see a picture of someone walking barefoot on the white-sand beaches of Hawaii, remember that beautiful sand is largely made from parrotfish poop. One parrotfish can poop out hundreds of pounds of sand in a year.

A group of barracuda is called a battery.

Captain James Cook carried a goat with him on his voyages to provide milk to his sailors. When the goat retired, she was given a silver collar as a reward for her years of service.

The Nile crocodile is the world's biggest reptile; the largest on record was 21 feet and 2 inches long and weighed over 2300 pounds.

Dolphins have names for each other.

In 2016, a sea lion pup wandered into a San Diego beachfront restaurant and took a seat in a booth by the window where he promptly took a little nap.

Bottlenose dolphins have been used by the U.S. military to detect enemy swimmers trying to plant bombs. Corporal Wojtek of the Polish army was a bear. He carried ammunition for Polish soldiers and was made an officer, so he could get special food and hang out with other officers.

The colossal squid has eyes the size of basketballs.

Dolphins enjoy getting high on the toxins produced by handling pufferfish.

The loudest animal in the world, the Pistol Shrimp, is only 2 cm long. This little prawn can snap its claw shut so fast that it creates a bubble that produces a sonic blast when it bursts, louder than the giant airplane the Concorde's sonic boom.

Sea otters sometimes use the pouches under their arms to carry snacks.

A blue whale's tongue weighs more than an entire elephant.

Even though most dolphins don't have a natural enemy, they sleep with one eye open - just in case.

Our Feathered Friends

The elf owl is a tiny bird that sometimes lives inside a cactus during the day.

A group of owls is called a parliament.

The ostrich is the largest bird in the world.

The chicken is the most common species of bird.

Christopher Columbus brought back two parrots for Queen Isabella when he returned from his voyage to America in 1492.

The swift, a soft-tailed blackbird, can fly for almost an entire year without landing

A group of ravens is called an "unkindness".
(Rather rude, I think.)

During World War I and World War 2, pigeons fitted with secret cameras were used to map military battlefields, territories and targets.

Although rare, there are completely white ravens. These birds often have blue eyes.

A recently hatched raven has to eat enough to increase its weight by 50% a day. Talk about a ravenous appetite!

A raven is a really large crow.

Of all animals, ravens behave in a way most similar to humans.

Homing pigeons have been used for thousands of years to carry messages.

According to tradition, 6 ravens must always live on the grounds of the Tower of London.

A group of crows is called a murder.

Hummingbirds can fly backwards.

Ravens enjoy hanging out with friends and relatives. By the way, did you know crows are thought to be the most intelligent of all birds? They can be easily tamed and taught to mimic human sounds. Crows also know how to use tools and will shape and use bits of wire, string, sticks and other objects to help fish out food from hard-to-reach places. To keep their tools from being stolen, a crow will hide them away or step on them when other birds are around.

The bird with the longest beak is the Australian Pelican. Its beak is about 50 centimeters (19.68 inches) long and makes up a quarter of its entire body length.

Parrots can hold food up to their beak while eating. They can grab it with one foot and then move it to their beak so they can nibble it.

The group names for ravens (an unkindness or treachery) probably came from mythology, where ravens were said to be bad luck and to be tricksters. These birds cleverly hide their food, mimic human voices, and communicate with each other about what's happening around them.

Not only can ravens copy human words, they can also mimic other noises, like toilets flushing, car engines, and other bird or animal sounds.

Ravens also use sophisticated gestures, holding objects or pointing with their beaks.

Ravens love to play, and have been seen rolling down snowy hills, and playing keep away with other animals like wolves, otters, and dogs. Sometimes they even make fun of other animals.

Parrots are amazingly smart; they can add, subtract, and understand the meaning of zero.

Parrots can learn to say hundreds of words.

An African Gray parrot named Alex has a vocabulary of around 100 words.

Parrots understand music and move to it, as if dancing to the tune.

Parrots enjoy preening themselves.

Parakeets can learn tricks.

Parakeets, who are often known as budgies, are part of the parrot family. They are basically little parrots.

A group of parrots is called a pandemonium.

The word parakeet means "long tail".

Parrots are loving creatures and often show their affection by touching beaks. A parrot might also do this to a human they like.

Parakeets can learn to mimic your words and will use this ability to get attention. Some parakeets can learn a large number of words. The world record for parakeet with the largest vocabulary goes to Gus, who knew 1,700 words.

Parrots often live 80 - 100 years. They are the longest-lived bird species.

Ducks like to surf and can be seen riding waves to shore.

Toucans curl into balls when they sleep.

Crows, ravens, parrots, and jays are the smartest birds.

Most scientists believe birds evolved from dinosaurs.

Most hummingbirds weigh less than a nickel.

An albatross can soar for up to 6 hours without moving its wings.

Bats use sound, similar to radar, to find food. They make high-pitched squeaks that bounce off objects, giving away their location.

Bats are only able to see at night.

Houseflies always buzz in the key of F.

Crows like to play tricks on each other.

Butterflies taste with their feet.

Ravens and crows can remember faces.

Birds have hollow bones that help them fly.

The bumblebee bat is the world's smallest mammal - body length 1.14 to 1.29 inches.

Seagulls stamp on the ground to fool worms into thinking it's raining. This tricks the worms into coming above ground.

Ravens protect the Tower of London.

Pirates Rule the Sea

Blackbeard, the most feared pirate of his time, would weave hemp into his beard and set it on fire right before he attacked another ship.

According to legend, pirates were given earrings to celebrate a successful voyage.

Long ago, some pirate ships had full-time bands to play sea shanties (a type of song usually sung by sailors).

Do you know what Blackbeard's real name was? Edward Teach. Once Edward became a pirate, it was probably a good idea to liven the name up a bit. Who could really be afraid of "The fearsome Eddie" or "The horrible Mr. Teach.".

America's first female pirate was a woman named Rachel Wall.

Pirates in movies and books seem to love drinking grog. It turns out this is an actual mixed drink made from rum, water, lemon juice, and sugar.

Pirate ships used different pictures on their flags. The Jolly Roger, which displayed the skull and crossbones, was the most popular.

Pirate John Rackham, commonly known as Calico Jack is most remembered for having two female crew members: Mary Read and Anne Bonny.

Flag of Pirate Calico Jack

If you were a pirate, stopping in the Bahamas, you might get a new flag made by a sail-maker's widow, who liked to be paid in brandy.

Some famous pirates were women. These included Mary Read, Ching Chih, Grace O'Malley, and Anne Bonny.

Ever wonder why pirates are shown wearing eye patches. This is not because they all got poked in the eye. The eye with the patch was always adjusted to darkness. This helped the pirate see at night or in the dim light below deck.

Pirate captains were elected by popular vote and the crew could remove the captain from office if he didn't do a good job.

Even though pirates were a wild group who acted well outside the law, they still had to abide by a code. If you wanted to sail with Bartholomew (Black Bart) Roberts, here are some of the rules you had to follow:

1. Every man shall have an equal vote.
2. Every man shall have an equal share of plunder, food and strong liquors.
3. If the pirate took more than his share, he would be taken off the ship and marooned.
4. If any man robbed another, his ears would be cut and he would be marooned.
5. No gambling with dice or cards.
6. Lights and candles must be out by 8 at night. (Who knew pirates had a bed time!).
7. Each man must keep his weapons clean and ready for action.
8. If you desert your post, you will be killed or marooned.
9. Don't fight on board the ship. Wait until you're on shore.
10. Musicians shall have rest on Sunday.

Pirates really did have pet parrots. The men could get them easily at ports in the Caribbean and sell the birds for a huge profit when they got back to London. Meanwhile, the pirates could keep their favorites as pets. The birds were colorful, friendly, easy to care for, and could be taught to talk. Lots of fun during the boring hours sailing the open seas.

The pirate Christopher Moody's flag was so fearsome and colorful, it became known as the Bloody Red.

High-ranking officers on pirate ships got their own rooms, but the rest of the crew slept in the large space below deck in hammocks. The hammocks would sway with the movement of the ship, gently rocking the pirates to sleep.

The local people were always happy to see the arrival of a pirate ship on their shores. Pirates might have been terrifying to other ships on the ocean, but they spent lots of money and contributed to the local economies of port towns. (Kind of like people on cruise ships - but with cutlasses and eye patches.)

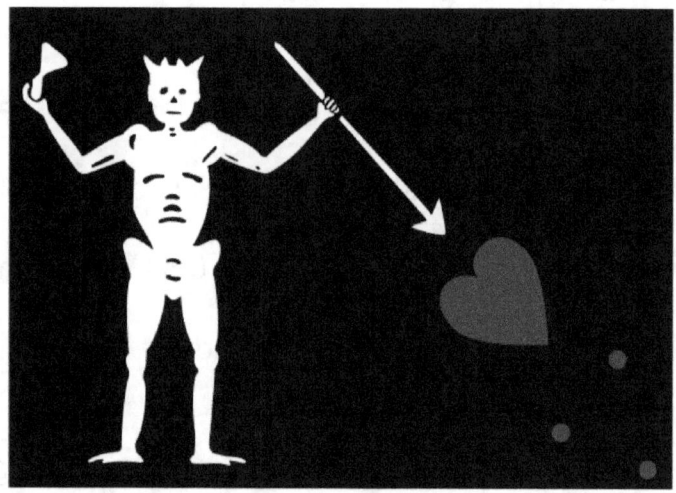

Blackbeard's Flag

Blackbeard got creative with his flag. The banner that hung from his mast featured a skeleton with horns, holding an hourglass in one hand and a spear in the other. The spear pointed to a heart dripping three drops of blood.

The famous Roman emperor, Julius Caesar, was taken prisoner by pirates when he was 25 years old. When the pirates demanded 20 talents (Roman money) ransom for his release, Caesar apparently laughed at them and told his captors to raise the price to 50. While waiting for the ransom to be paid, Caesar forced the pirates to listen to long speeches and bad poetry he had made up. When the money was handed over, the pirates, true to their word, released Julius Caesar. (I bet they were happy to get rid of him.)

Remarkable Inventions

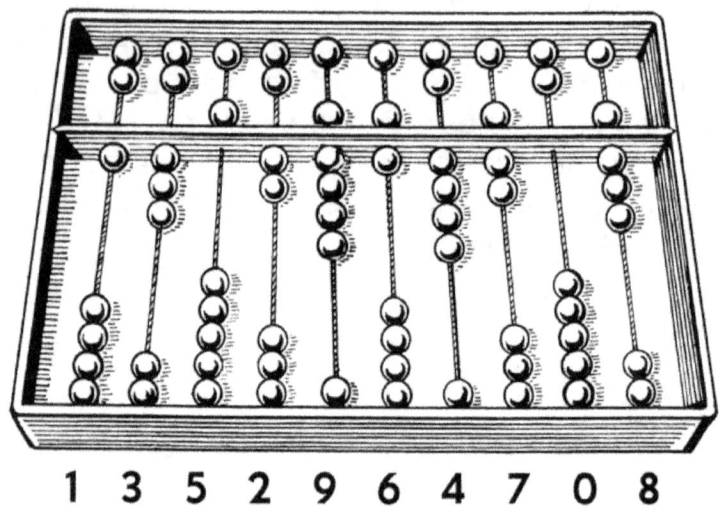

1 3 5 2 9 6 4 7 0 8

The counting device called the abacus was invented in Babylonia in 2400 BC.

Whitcomb Judson came up with the idea of the zipper in 1892.

Boomerangs were originally used thousands of years ago in Australia as hunting weapons.

Galileo Galilei came up with the ideas for the thermometer, telescope, and compass.

In 2009, an alarm to warn deaf people about a fire was invented. When it's triggered by smoke, the alarm releases a powerful smell of wasabi horseradish.
In 2007, a woman invented a bra that could be turned into two gas masks.

Velcro was invented after a scientist noticed a type of seed sticking to his dog's fur after a hike.

Laszlo Biro invented the first ballpoint pen in 1938. In Britain, some people refer to a ballpoint pen as a Biro.

The first cell phone was created in 1973 and weighed 4.5 lbs. (Try putting that in your backpack or pocket.)

Thomas Edison had over 1000 patents in his name. It seems he stole the ideas for many of them.

The barcodes found on products from oranges to refrigerators were first designed in 1949, and are based on the dots and dashes of Morse Code.

Nikola Tesla invented the first remote control using radio waves in 1898.

In 1867, A man named Luke Moon invented the butter stick.

The rubber band was invented in 1845 by a man named Stephen Perry.

The crossword puzzle was invented in 1913 by a journalist named Arthur Wynne.

The flushing toilet was invented by Sir John Harrington, the godson of Queen Elizabeth I. He installed the first working model in her bathroom.

Thomas Edison invented the phonograph, which could record and play back sound. In 1877, he made the world's first recording. The song he chose for this occasion was "Mary Had a Little Lamb".

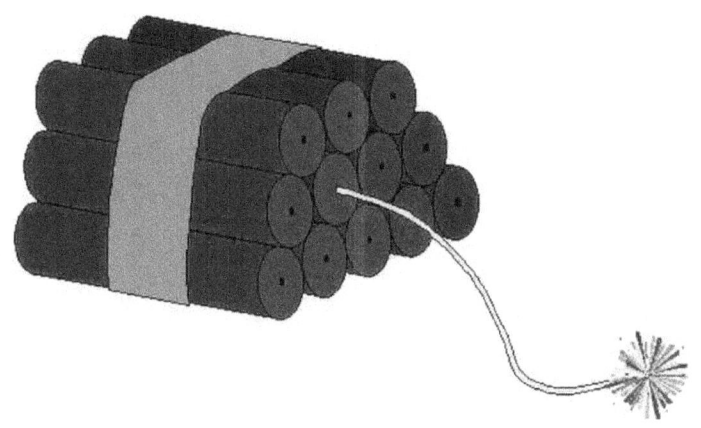

Alfred Nobel (the guy the Nobel Peace Prize is named for) created dynamite in 1867.

The first sealed can to keep food preserved was invented in 1810. The first can opener was invented in 1858 - 48 years later. Opening cans must have been tough during those years.

Sir Francis Bacon invented frozen chicken in 1626. However, he died from a chill he got while testing freezing methods. (Perhaps he should have put the *chicken* in the freezer.)

The first mechanical computer was invented by Charles Babbage in 1822; he called it his *difference engine*.

It was in 2003 that dogs and their owners could both stay dry during a walk in the rain. In October of this year the combination dog leash and umbrella was patented.

The toaster was originally invented to make stale bread taste good enough to eat.

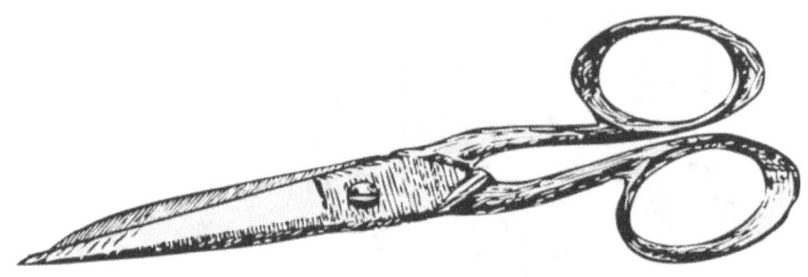

Leonardo da Vinci invented scissors.

The first matches were created by John Walker in 1826; he called them *friction lights*.

The CIA developed the "insectohopter" in 1974. This remote-controlled device looked like a dragonfly and could secretly record conversations. Unfortunately, its miniature engine ran out of gas in about a minute. This invention never made it to the big time, but it could be said the "insectohopter" was the first ever drone.

Ben Franklin invented bifocals, the lightning rod and a musical instrument called the armonica.

The first baby stroller, invented in 1733, was designed to be pulled by a goat.

Displayed in the International Spy Museum in Washington, DC, is a spy weapon nicknamed "The Kiss of Death." This device looks like a simple lipstick, but is, in fact, a tiny pistol, capable of shooting one bullet.

How about this for another cool invention? A bicycle for spies that will recharge a portable radio while the rider pedals.

Ever heard of doggles? These stylish glasses are made to fit the shape of a dog's head and protect its eyes from dirt and dust.

Cat videos have a long history. After inventing the kinetograph (early movie recorder) in 1892, Thomas Edison recorded videos of cute boxing cats. (You can even watch these on YouTube.)

Sports and Games

An American woman named Diana Nyad swam 110 miles, all the way from Cuba to Florida without stopping. She was 64 years old at the time.

Honey has been used as the center for golf balls.

Wayne Gretzky won 9 hockey Most Valuable Player awards, three more than any other player.

Romanian gymnast, Nadia Comaneci was the first gymnast (and youngest) to be awarded a perfect 10 in any Olympic gymnastics event. She was 14 years old.

In 1962, basketball great Wil Chamberlain scored 100 points in a single game.

The baseball pitcher, Cy Young, holds the major league records for complete games (749). During his 22-year career he also established world records for wins, losses and number if innings pitched. It's no wonder a famous Major League Baseball award is named after him.

The longest Major League Baseball game ever played lasted 25 innings and went on for eight hours and six minutes of playing time.

The largest blowout in National League Football history was when the Chicago Bears trounced the Washington Redskins 73-0.

The longest hitting streak in baseball is still held by Joe DiMaggio, who got a hit in 56 straight games.

On a day in December 1891, a gym teacher named James Naismith, who worked at the YMCA in Springfield Massachusetts, was told by his boss to invent a game the boys could play inside, during the long winter, when it was too cold to go out. Naismith gave this some thought. Finally, he nailed a peach basket to the balcony on either side of the gym, came up with a few rules, and the game of basketball was born.

The longest tennis match in history was in June 2010 between John Isner and Nicolas Mahut. It lasted 11 hours and 5 minutes.

The one country that has competed in all the Olympic games under its own flag is (you guessed it) Greece.

Check out the Surfer Dog!

Dog surfing is a sport that began in California during the 1920s. The goal is pretty straightforward - a dog rides a surfboard. The dog that stays on the board longest wins. (Obviously, the owners are around to make sure their dogs stay safe.)

Princess Anne, the daughter of Queen Elizabeth II, competed as an equestrian in the 1976 Olympic games.

Michael Phelps has won more medals than any other Olympian with 28, a record 23 of those are gold. He is the most decorated Olympian of all time.

Jamaican sprinter Usain Bolt is the fastest man on earth.

The first competitive sport was most likely wrestling, which began in Greece in 776 BC. Other sports that began around the same time were running and javelin throwing.

Modern Olympic Gold medals are made mostly from sterling silver, not gold. They haven't been made of pure gold since 1912.

Ski ballet was, for a brief time, an Olympic sport.

Major league baseball umpires have to wear black underwear, just in case their pants rip.

Between 1900 and 1920, Tug-Of-War was an Olympic sport.

The average person takes enough steps during their lifetime to walk around the world four times.

Two sports have been played in outer space. Astronaut Alan Shepherd hit a golf ball and another astronaut, Edgar Mitchell, threw a javelin as they stood on the moon in 1971.

Traditionally, jockeys used to get paid in coins, no matter how much they earned.

The game of volleyball was invented in 1895 in Massachusetts, US.

Bowling was invented around 3200 BC in Egypt. Minoru Yoshida from Japan set the world record for most push-ups in a row - 10,507.

Here's a record for you... In order to raise money for two anti-bullying charities, Ben Smith of the UK ran 401 marathons in 401 days.

The longest boxing match in history was fought in 1893 and went on for over seven hours.

London, UK is the only city to have hosted the Olympics three times: 1908, 1948, 2012.

The first hang glider was built in 1890 and was made out of wood and cloth.

Half of the American population doesn't know how to swim.

Between 1982 and 1987, Martina Navratilova won six Wimbledon titles in a row.

Hopscotch is one of the many children's games that began in ancient times. Old records exist that show Roman children and Roman soldiers playing a variation of this sidewalk and playground game.

Welsh Town in Wales in home of one of the more peculiar sporting competitions. Once a year, men and horses compete against each other in a 22-mile marathon. Needless to say, the horses usually win.

In Kenya, they have a race called "To Hell's Gate on a Wheelbarrow", which is named after the national park. The race is held to raise funds that go to conservation efforts for the park.

The first bumper cars hit amusement parks in 1920.

In the early days of baseball, umpires would recline in rocking chairs 20 feet (6 meters) behind home plate.

Soccer is the most watched sport in the world.

Strange Bits of History

Abraham Lincoln believed in ghosts and consulted mediums while in the White House. He felt the messages he received from the spirit world helped him through many of the crises he faced as president.

President Lincoln lives on in the White House.

Witnesses from First Lady Eleanor Roosevelt to Queen Wilhelmina of the Netherlands, from President Theodore Roosevelt to President Ronald Reagan all saw or sensed the presence of Abraham Lincoln while in the White House.

Famed rock group The Beatles arranged seances where they communicated with their dead manager Brian Epstein.

Knitting was originally only done by men.

Mary Queen of Scots was only six days old when she became queen of Scotland in 1542.

The famous London Clock, "Big Ben", chimed for the first time on 11 July, 1859.

People once ate arsenic to improve their skin.

The Great Pyramid of Giza is made of more than 2 million blocks of stone. Each stone weighs 2.5 tons. That's a lot of weight to move around, especially with nothing more advanced than barges, heavy sleds and oxen. (Some people think the ancient builders were helped by aliens from outer space.)

All British armored vehicles come with the equipment needed to make tea.

Romans protected their homes with guard dogs and even had "Beware of the Dog" signs.

Alexander the Great named over 70 cities after himself.

The Great pyramid was the tallest man-made structure in the world for over 3,800 years and is the oldest of the *Seven Wonders of the Ancient World*.

Before the invention of the alarm clock, people would pay someone to wake them up. The individuals who did this were called "knocker-uppers". People would hire these helpers to "knock them up" at a specific time.

Animals are sensitive to vibrations of the earth. In 1975 the Chinese city of Haicheng was evacuated 2 hours before an earthquake when they noticed their animals behaving oddly.

The great general Napoleon was attacked by bunnies while hunting and had to flee.

Theodore Roosevelt had a pet hyena named Bill.

In 1866, the country of Lichtenstein sent out an army of eighty men to fight in the Austro-Prussian War. None of the eighty soldiers were injured; eighty-one returned, including a "new Italian friend".

The Romans made hamburgers and ate takeout food.

The longest war was fought between France and England and lasted for 116 years.

Confederate General "Stonewall" Jackson was mistakenly killed by his own men.

The Ancient Egyptians used specially curved stones as pillows.

Cleopatra was not Egyptian; the famous beauty, and ruler of ancient Egypt, was actually Greek.

Roman homes had central heating.

President Abraham Lincoln was a wrestler and was elected to the Wrestling Hall of Fame.

No witches were burned during the Salem Witch Trials. Some were jailed and a few were hanged – but none was burned.

President Andrew Jackson had a parrot named Polly who loved to swear.

The shortest war in history was fought between Britain and Zanzibar. It lasted 38 minutes.

In England, during the 1700s and 1800s, pineapples were thought of as a status symbol. People who were rich enough to own one would display it in their homes and carry it with them to show how wealthy and high-class they were.

The most popular pets among Romans were ferrets, dogs, and monkeys.

Tablecloths were originally used as one giant, shared napkin.

The sweat of gladiators was sometimes mixed into skincare products in ancient Rome.

Here's another one from those wacky Romans. The ancient Romans often used stale urine as mouthwash.

President Lincoln was a licensed bartender.

Remember the children's rhyme, "Mary Had a Little Lamb"? It turns out there was a real Mary, and she really had a little lamb. And, yes, it followed her to school one day. The poem was written to Mary by a boy named John Roulstone, who went to school with her.

The Roman Emperor Caligula made his horse a senator.

The South African railway once employed a baboon to operate signals. He did not make one mistake in his entire career.

Superstitions

An old superstition in Mexico warns against putting two mirrors in front of each other - it opens a door for the devil.

In the Philippines mourners stop off at a coffee shop or fast-food place before going home from a funeral. Apparently, you need to "shake off" the bad spirits to keep them away from your home. But how about those innocent, now-haunted coffee shops and MacDonalds?

In China and Japan, you must never stick your chopsticks straight down into your food as this will invite death.

In many countries you mustn't whistle indoors or you will summon the devil.

In the United States, Australia, Canada, and the United Kingdom, Friday 13th is thought to be unlucky. However, in many Spanish-speaking countries, Friday the 13th is a lucky day, while Tuesday the 13th is unlucky. The name of the horror film series, "Friday the 13th" was changed to "Tuesday the 13th" when it was translated into Spanish.

If you sing during dinner in the Netherlands, you are said to be thanking the devil and praising him for your food.

An Argentinian superstition warns that the seventh son will turn into a werewolf.

Many people all over the world believe it is bad luck to open an umbrella indoors. (Perhaps that's just common sense. You don't want to poke someone in the eye with one of those pointy pieces.)

According to Turkish legend, when you chew gum at night, it turns into the flesh of the dead. (Yikes! That's disgusting.)

Spilling salt is thought to be bad luck. However, throwing a pinch of salt over your left shoulder reverses the curse. Depending on the country you're from, either the devil, or evil spirits lurk just behind your left shoulder. Therefore, throwing salt in that direction blinds the evil character and makes him helpless.

In France, if you step in dog poop with your left foot, it's considered good luck.

There's a superstition in Canada that expectant mothers who crave fish but don't eat it will end up having a baby with a fish head. Wow! I can't imagine what the baby would look like if the mother wanted a pizza and didn't get one.

Back in medieval times, ladders were associated with the gallows. This is why, in many countries, it's considered bad luck to walk under one. But what do you do if you realize you've accidentally violated this superstition? Just walk backwards through the ladder again and you'll be fine.

In many cultures, a horseshoe is a remarkably lucky symbol, and if you find one with the open end pointing in your direction, you'll have an especially lucky day.

Irish brides deck themselves out with bells to ward off evil spirits that might ruin their wedding day.

In the United States, many people hold the superstition that it's bad luck to have a black cat cross your path. In the UK, Japan, and Australia, the opposite is true. A black cat crossing your path is a sign of good luck and good fortune. If a black cat shows up at your door, invite it in; the cat is a sign that good luck and prosperity are heading your way.

Lucky Black Cat

Pirates and other sailors would keep a black cat on their ships as they believed it would bring good luck.

In Japan, it is believed that a bride will be happy in her marriage if a black cat sneezes on her wedding day.

One Japanese superstition warns you not to cut your fingernails after dark - or you could cause an early death.

In Turkey, it is believed if you jump over a child, he or she will be short forever.

Here's one... if you kiss a baby on the lips, the child will drool for the rest of its life.

"Knock on wood" is a common way of warding off evil, especially after you've said something positive. "I'm going to have a great day." (Knock wood.)

Broken Mirror

Breaking a mirror will cause 7 years of bad luck. It is said you can reverse the curse by putting all the pieces in a container and burying them under the light of the moon. (But be very careful picking up the pieces.)

The Human Body

You cannot lick your elbow... go ahead, try.

You can't taste when your tongue is completely dry.

Children have better hearing than adults.

A human sneeze can travel 100 miles per hour.

Your Ears Will Never Get This Big

Even when the rest of your body stops growing, your ears and nose continue to get bigger.

The biggest muscle is the gluteus maximus, or butt muscle. In Latin, "gluteus" means buttock and "maximus" means largest.

The most common eye color is brown.

The funny bone is not a bone; it's a sensitive nerve near your elbow.

Blood cells are made inside your bones.

You have more than 600 muscles in your body.

Fingernails grow faster on the hand the person uses the most.

Only 2% of people in the world have green eyes.

Only 2% of people are naturally blond.

You get a new outer layer of skin every 30 days.

The average person farts 14 times a day.

Your brain is made up of 85% water - the same as a cabbage.

About 10% of the world is left-handed. About 1 percent are able to use both hands equally (ambidextrous).

Every human has a unique tongue print.

An adult human has 206 bones in their body. Over half of these are in the feet (52 bones) and hands (54 bones).

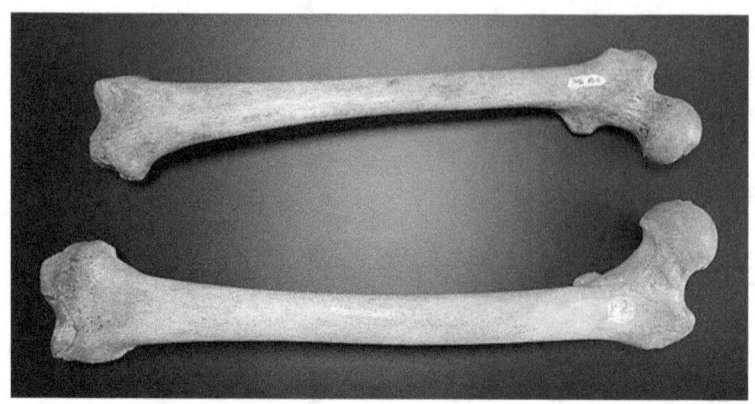

Femurs (Thigh Bones)

The longest bone in your body is the femur, also called the thigh bone. It's also the strongest. This bone makes up almost a quarter of your full height.

The smallest bone in your body is called the stapes, and it's located in the ear. This tiny bone is only 0.1 inches (2.54 millimeters) long.

Bones can repair themselves if they get broken.

The fastest muscles in the human body are the ones that make your eyes blink.

The average human heart beats about 100,000 times per day.

The word muscle comes from the Latin word meaning "little mouse".

Stomach acid is so strong, it can dissolve metal.

Bodies give off a tiny amount of light that's too weak for the human eye to see.

Human teeth are just as strong as shark teeth.

Fingernails grow four times faster than toenails.

Laughter reduces allergic reactions.

The adult heart weighs less than 1 pound.

Laughing is good for your heart.

The circulatory system is more than 60,000 miles long.

The average length of time a person can hold their breath is 30 to 90 seconds. The world record is 19 minutes and 30 seconds - recorded by a Dane named Stig Severinsen under water. A person can hold their breath twice as long underwater as they can on land.

The top running speed for a human being was set by Usain Bolt during the 100-meter sprint at the World Championships in 2009. He finished the race in 9.58 seconds - 23.3 miles per hour. By comparison, the average healthy man can run this distance at 5.9 miles per hour.

Florence Griffith-Joyner

The world record holding fastest woman sprinter is Florence Griffith-Joyner, who ran the 100-meter dash in 10.49 seconds - 21.32 miles per hour. The average healthy female can run it at 5.0 miles per hour.

Blood is as salty as seawater.
A blood cell zooms around the body in about 45 seconds.

Human beings have two ears so they can tell which direction sound is coming from.

In order to make room for your heart, your left lung is smaller than your right.

Urine is mostly water, and can be drunk in an emergency. (That would have to be some big emergency! Yuck!)

More men than women are color blind.

Only humans blush.

People spend about a third of their lives sleeping.

Human yawns are contagious, even to cats and dogs.

Some people have been known to text in their sleep.

According to NASA, the perfect nap lasts 26 minutes.

It's impossible to sneeze while you're asleep.

Where is it? Where did it Happen?

The world's smallest country is Vatican City in Rome.

The Crown Jewels of the United Kingdom are on display at the Tower of London.

Mount Rushmore

Mount Rushmore National Memorial is a huge sculpture carved into the side of a mountain in South Dakota. The sculpture displays images of four U.S. presidents: George Washington, Thomas Jefferson, Theodore Roosevelt, and Abraham Lincoln.

The Mount Rushmore monument is 60 feet high and each president's head is the size of a 6-story building.

The largest snowball fight on record took place in Seattle, Washington - 5,834 people participated.

The longest international border is between Canada and the United States.

The largest country in the world is Russia.

Tibet is the highest region in the world.

There is one vending machine for every 40 people in Japan.

In Saudi Arabia, you will find solar-powered pay phones.

The first diamond found in South Africa was picked up by children on the beach.

In 1492, when Christopher Columbus and his men on the Nina, the Pinta and Santa Maria, finally set foot on land after a long sea voyage, he thought they'd landed in Asia. Actually, Christopher and his men had reached the shores of what is now called the Bahamas.

The U.S. state of Arizona has the most telescopes in the world.

The world's shortest river is only 67 yards long.

The U.S. has one active diamond mine; it's located in Arkansas.

The highest tides in the world can be found in Canada's Bay of Fundy. High tides here can reach 56 feet, taller than a five-story building. At low tide, people can walk along the ocean floor, but they must be careful not to get caught out there when the tide comes in.

Boring, Oregon and Dull, Scotland have been sister cities since 2012.

Canada has more lakes than any other country - 879,800 to be exact.

California is the only U.S. state to have hosted both the summer and winter Olympics.

The state of Hawaii has its own time zone.

The Philippines consists of 7,641 islands.

The world's tallest mountain is Mount Everest in the Himalayas

The first to reach the top? On May 29th, 1953, Edmund Hillary of New Zealand and Tenzing Norgay of Nepal became the first two people to reach the top of Mt. Everest.

The world's oldest subway system is the London Underground in England.

The London Underground was originally built in 1863. It has grown over the years and now has 250 miles of track and 275 stations.

In 1911, the Norwegian explorer, Roald Amundsen, led the first expedition all the way to the South Pole.

The world's longest railroad is the Trans-Siberian Railway. It is more than 5,770 miles along and runs all the way across Russia, from Moscow to Vladivostok.

A one-way trip of the Trans-Siberian railway involves crossing 3,901 bridges.

Siberia's Lake Baikal is 5,250 feet deep, making it the deepest lake in the world. It's also one of the biggest. Lake Baikal is so big, it contains as much water as all five of North America's Great Lakes put together.

The Grand Canyon in Arizona is the world's largest canyon.

The highest mountain in Greece is Mount Olympus. The ancient Greeks believed the 12 most important gods and goddesses lived at the top of this great mountain.

The surface of Mars is icy cold.

The Sahara Desert covers an area about the size of the United States.

Greenland is the largest island in the world.
Canada has 6 time zones.

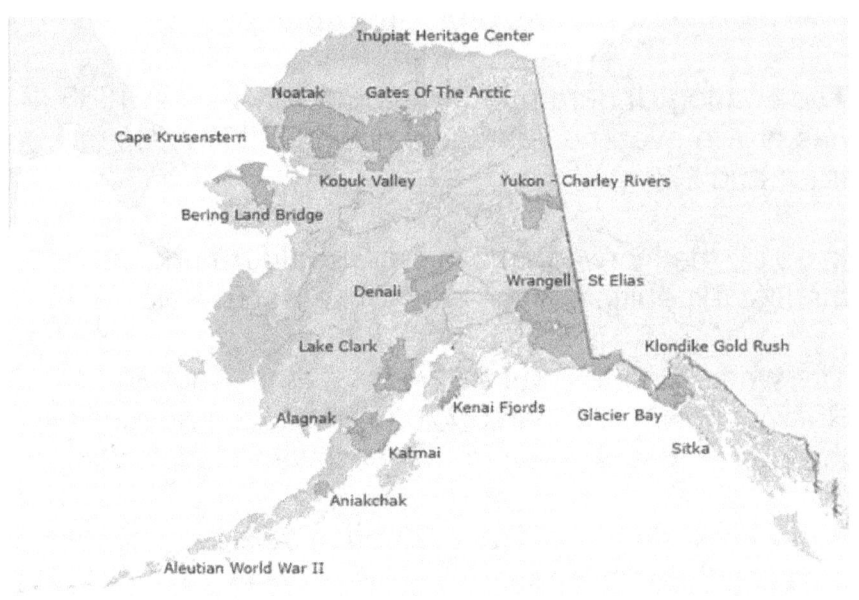

Russia sold Alaska to the United States for about 2 cents per acre.

Weird Museums

Most of us have heard of museums like the London Museum, the Museum of Modern Art in New York, or the Louvre in France with their displays of famous pictures and historical artifacts. But there are also some more unusual museums out there to be explored.

If you happen to be visiting England, you can stop by and take a look around the Dog Collar Museum, the Lawn Mower Museum or possibly the Cumberland Pencil Museum.

Close to half a million visitors a year tour the Dog Collar Museum.

In the Lawn Mower Museum, you'll find a working lawn mower less than 5 centimeters (1.98 inches) high.

And in the Cumberland Pencil Museum, you will find everything from secret spy pencils to a tour of a real pencil factory.

The state of Minnesota has a museum with exhibits dedicated to the canned meat called SPAM.

Burlingame, California is home to the world's only PEZ museum where you can see the world's largest PEZ dispenser standing proudly at 7 feet 10 inches high.

If you like weird museums, with this one you're in for a treat. In India, you can stop by the Sulabh International Museum of Toilets.

In England, you can tour Alnwick Garden, the most dangerous garden in the world. It's a unique place dedicated only to plants that can kill you. To enter, you must pass through an iron gate that has a warning sign displaying a skull and crossbones.

Back in the United States, you will find the Museum of Failed Products and the Kansas Barbed Wire Museum.

The city of Beijing in China has a museum dedicated to the history of water taps, including 130 real objects.

Be sure to pack a lunch when you visit the Museum of Bread Culture in Germany. This museum has more than 18,000 exhibits all about bread, but not a single slice you can eat.

Another collection of the weird can be found at the Button Museum located off the highway in South Carolina. Here you will find shoes, suits, guitars, hats, and more all covered in buttons. The true button fan can even buy a CD filled with songs about... you guessed it, buttons.

You might want to visit the Yo-Yo Museum in Chino, California where you can watch demonstrations of advanced Yo-Yo techniques, learn the history of the Yo-Yo and see over 3,000 exhibits dedicated to this enduring toy.

Finally, there's the Museum of Bad Art located next to the toilets in an old basement in Dedham, Massachusetts. This museum will only display art that is so bad it "wouldn't make it to your mother's fridge".

Words and Language

E is the most commonly used letter in the English language. (This little fact has been used to help crack difficult codes.)

In 1825, a blind Frenchman, Louis Braille, developed a language that could be read by blind people.

English is said to be one of the happiest languages in the world - and the word "happy" is used 3 times more often than the word "sad".

The United States has no official language.

More words in English begin with *s* than any other letter. (Also good for code cracking)

The most commonly used consonants are *r* and *t*.

One-fourth of the world's population speaks at least some English.

The word alphabet comes from the first two letters of the Greek alphabet, "alpha" and "beta".

The Roman alphabet had 23 letters. Missing were *J,V,* and *W.* (Although V was a number)

I is the shortest word in the English language and the oldest. It's also the most common word used in conversation.

Q is the only letter not in the name of a U.S. state.

Only two English words end in "-gry" - hungry and angry.

No and Go are two of the shortest complete sentences.

The butterfly was originally called a flutterby.

The word checkmate in chess comes from the Persian phrase "Shah Mat" meaning "the king is helpless."

One word in the English language has no true vowels: rhythm.

The letter V is never silent.

The is the most common English word.

Scotland has 421 words for snow.

At one time, the ampersand (&) was considered the 27th letter of the English language.

In the United States, the letter *z* is pronounced zee, but it's pronounced zed in the United Kingdom.
The library of Congress is the largest library in the world.

The opposite of "sparkle" is "darkle". (The word 'darkle' means to grow dark or to become clouded and gloomy.)

The word "fizzle" originally meant to "break wind quietly".

The word "whatever" consistently tops the list of the most annoying words in English.

In 2016, the granddaughter of a U.K. man who had failed to return a library book from a school library returned it 120 years after it had been borrowed. The library let her slide on paying the overdue fine.

The oldest library in the world was in the country of Assyria (now known as Iraq). It was founded in the seventh century BC and the "books" were actually stone tablets.

The Great Library of Alexandria in Egypt was established in 295 BC, and the "books" it contained were thousands and thousands of papyrus scrolls.

Some libraries allow patrons to borrow items other than books; DVDs, audio books, tools, telescopes, and baking supplies are just a few of these items.

On average, people go to the library three times more often than they go to the movies.

4,000 English words are added to the dictionary each year.

Bookkeeper is the only English word with no hyphens that has three double letters in a row.

This sentence uses all 26 letters: "The quick brown fox jumps over the lazy dog."

The United States has no official language.

The adjective used most often in English is "good". The most frequently used noun is "time".

Month, orange, silver, and purple do not rhyme with any other word.

English is the official language of 67 countries.

The only word in English that ends with "mt" is dreamt.

There are seven ways to spell the sound "ee" in English. The following sentence contains them all. "He believed Caesar could see people seizing the seas."

Challenge Your Family and Friends
(Answers to All These Questions Can be Found in the Book)

Challenge #1
Animals

1. Where did the French Poodle originally come from?
   a. Germany
   b. Paris, France
   c. Poddle Village in England

2. What is a group of ravens called?
   a. A following
   b. An unkindness
   c. A crowning

3. What animal ran for Mayor of Mexico City in 2013?
   a. A bull
   b. A Chihuahua dog
   c. A cat

4. What is a polydactyl cat?
   a. A cat with an extra paw
   b. A cat with extra toes
   c. A cat that speaks several languages

5. Which animal needs the most sleep?
   a. Koalas
   b. House cats
   c. Sloths

6. Which of these animals has learned how to surf?
   a. Goats
   b. Horses
   c. Beavers

7. The smell of skunk spray is so powerful it can be smelled how far away?
   a. 20 miles
   b. 4 city blocks
   c. 3 miles

8. Who invented the first cat door?
   a. Sir Isaac Newton
   b. The Mattel toy company
   c. Leonardo da Vince

9. What country has the most cats per person?
   a. The United States
   b. Australia
   c. New Zealand

10.   What is a cats strongest sense?
   d. Smell
   e. Sight
   f. Touch

Challenge #2
Science

1. Wind power:
   a. Has been used for thousands of years
   b. Will start being used in 10 years
   c. Is dangerous

2. Why do stars appear to twinkle?
   a. They reflect moonlight
   b. Changes in the earth's atmosphere
   c. Stars are made of hard glass

3. There's no sound on the moon because:
   a. No one is there to hear
   b. There is no air to carry sound
   c. It has no gravity

4. Distances between stars are measured in:
   a. Light Years
   b. Miles
   c. Thousands of kilometers

5. How many people have walked on the surface of the moon?
   a. Two
   b. Six
   c. Twelve

6. Where is the largest population of camels found?
   a. Tasmania
   b. Arabia
   c. Australia

7. What is the hardest substance in the world?
    a. Elephant tusks
    b. Diamonds
    c. Shark's teeth

8. What is the only planet not named after a god?
    a. Earth
    b. Pluto
    c. Uranus

9. How long did the longest earthquake last?
    a. 6 hours
    b. 2 months
    c. 38 days

10.   What is the largest desert on earth?
    a. Sahara
    b. Gobi
    c. Arctic

Challenge #3
Inventions

1. What counting device was invented in Babylonia?
   - a. Fingers
   - b. Pocket calculator
   - c. Abacus

2. What are doggles?
   - a. Glasses to be used when skiing
   - b. Eye protection used during WW II
   - c. Glasses for dogs

3. Who invented the remote control?
   - a. Thomas Edison
   - b. Nikola Tesla
   - c. Steve Jobs

4. Who was the first person to make a cat video?
   - a. Thomas Edison
   - b. Sir Isaac Newton
   - c. Steven Spielberg

5. What were matches first called?
   - a. Igniters
   - b. Friction Lights
   - c. Hot Sticks

6. Which was invented first, the sealed can or the can opener?
   - a. The can
   - b. The can opener
   - c. Both were invented at the same time

7. What was the first mechanical computer called?
   a. The Univac
   b. The Maniac
   c. The Difference Engine

8. What is the spy weapon known as the "Kiss of Death"?
   a. Poison lipstick
   b. A tiny gun that looks like lipstick
   c. A vampire

9. When was the zipper invented?
   a. The 1500ds
   b. The 1800ds
   c. The 1950s

10.   What was the first song Edison recorded on his phonograph?
   a. The Minute Walz
   b. Happy Birthday
   c. Mary Had a Little Lamb

Challenge #4
Our Feathered Friends

1. What is the most common species of bird?
   a. Pigeon
   b. Sparrow
   c. Chicken

2. What is the largest bird in the world?
   a. The Emu
   b. The Ostrich
   c. The Trumpeter Swan

3. How long can a soft-tailed blackbird fly without landing?
   a. Three days
   b. Ten days
   c. Almost a year

4. What is a group of crows called?
   a. A murder
   b. A meeting
   c. An unkindness

5. What is the world's record for the largest vocabulary of a parakeet?
   a. 1,700 Words
   b. 50 Words
   c. As many words as a third grader

6. What is a group of parrots called?
   a. A quarrel
   b. A pandemonium
   c. A chatter

7. What kind of birds are always kept at the Tower of London?
   a. Swans
   b. Robins
   c. Ravens

8. Which type of bird can fly backwards?
   a. albatross
   b. Small ostrich
   c. Hummingbird

9. What is the world's smallest mammal?
   a. Bumblebee bat
   b. Humming bat
   c. Mini Eagle

10.   What do you call a group of owls?
   a. A tower
   b. A Parliament
   c. An Academy

Challenge #5
Strange History

1. How long was the longest war in known history?
   a. 100 years
   b. 214 years
   c. 116 years

2. Abraham Lincoln excelled in what sport?
   a. Swimming
   b. Badminton
   c. Wrestling

3. The shortest war in history was fought between Britain and Zanzibar. How long did it last?
   a. 38 minutes
   b. 11 weeks
   c. 6 hours

4. Which of these animals was not a pet of President Theodore Roosevelt?
   a. A bear
   b. A hyena
   c. A tiger cub

5. Which fruit was a sign of wealth in England in the 1700s?
   a. Apricots
   b. Pineapples
   c. Coconuts

6. What popular food was first eaten by the Romans?
   a. Macaroni and cheese
   b. Hamburgers
   c. Spaghetti

7. Which of these could be found in a Roman home?
    a. Air conditioning
    b. Ceiling fans
    c. Central heating

8. What nationality was Cleopatra?
    a. Egyptian
    b. Greek
    c. Roman

9. What did the ancient Egyptians use as pillows?
    a. Olive branches
    b. Woven papyrus
    c. Curved stones

10.   What animal once worked for the South African railway?
    a. A baboon
    b. A Bloodhound
    c. An Elephant

Answers to the Challenges

Challenge #1
1. Germany
2. An unkindness
3. A cat
4. A car with extra toes
5. Koalas
6. Goats
7. Three miles
8. Sir Isaac Newton
9. New Zealand
10.   Smell

Challenge #2
1. Has been used for thousands of years
2. Changes in earth's atmosphere
3. There is no air to carry sound
4. Light years
5. Twelve
6. Australia
7. Diamonds
8. Earth
9. 38 days
10.   Arctic

Challenge #3
1. Abacus
2. Glasses for dogs
3. Nikola Tesla
4. Thomas Edison
5. Friction lights
6. The can
7. The Difference Engine
8. A tiny gun that looks like lipstick
9. The 1800ds
10.   Mary had a little lamb

Challenge #4
1. Chicken
2. The Ostrich
3. Almost a year
4. Murder
5. 1,700 Words
6. A pandemonium
7. Ravens
8. Hummingbird
9. Bumblebee bat
10.   A parliament

Challenge #5
1. 116 years
2. Wrestling
3. 38 minutes
4. A tiger cub
5. Pineapples
6. Hamburger
7. Central heating
8. Greek
9. Curved stones
10.   A baboon

INDEX

146

I hope you enjoyed this book and discovered some new and interesting information.

If you did, I would love it if you could leave me a review.

If you would like to be emailed when I release my next book, please write to the address below. I would love to hear from you.

OldTownPublishing@gmail.com

HTTPS://OLDTOWNPUBLISHING.COM

www.ingramcontent.com/pod-product-compliance
Lightning Source LLC
Chambersburg PA
CBHW071153120626
46546CB00006B/2252